A Gift for You Compliments of

Trafford Library
416 Brinton Ave.
Trafford, PA 15085
412-372-5115

ANGELS, DEMONS, AND RELIGIOUS RITUALS

ELDORADO INK

The Supernatural

Witches and Wicca

Haunted Places and Ghostly Encounters

New Orleans Voodoo

Shamans, Witch Doctors, Wizards, Sorcerers, and Alchemists

The Undead: Vampires, Zombies, and other Strange Monsters

Legendary Creatures

Unexplained Monsters and Cryptids

Angels, Demons, and Religious Rituals

THE SUPERNATURAL

ANGELS, DEMONS, AND RELIGIOUS RITUALS

BY AUDREY ALEXANDER

ELDORADO INK

Eldorado Ink
PO Box 100097
Pittsburgh, PA 15233
www.eldoradoink.com

Produced by OTTN Publishing, Stockton, New Jersey

CPSIA compliance information: Batch#S2015.
For further information, contact Eldorado Ink at info@eldoradoink.com.

First printing

1 3 5 7 9 8 6 4 2

Library of Congress Cataloging-in-Publication Data

   Applied for
      ISBN 978-1-61900-065-0 (hc)
      ISBN 978-1-61900-073-5 (trade)
      ISBN 978-1-61900-081-0 (ebook)

*For information about custom editions, special sales, or premiums,
please contact our special sales department at info@eldoradoink.com.*

TABLE OF CONTENTS

The Exorcism of Sister Madeleine

In 1610, a young French nun began to exhibit strange behavior. Screaming obscenities. Shaking and crying. Neighing like a horse. Demonic visions. Was Sister Madeleine insane? A criminal? A local priest had another explanation—she was possessed by a demon. And he was ready to perform an exorcism to save her soul.

A Nun Possessed

Father Louis Gaufridi got more than he bargained for when he was called in to banish the devil from Sister Madeleine and another possessed nun, named Louise. Fearing that news of the devil in the local convent would scare townspeople, Father Gaufridi tried to keep the strange behavior of the nuns a secret. He tried performing an exorcism rite, even though Sister Madeleine claimed she wasn't possessed.

But rumors of devilish behavior at the convent in Aix-en-Provence continued. Other nuns accused Madeleine of falling down in fits that contorted her body. It was rumored that she had even destroyed a cru-

A French bishop expels a demon from a woman in this Medieval painting from the cathedral at Bayeux. Exorcism is the name for a ritual by which evil spirits or demons are forced to abandon humans they have possessed.

cifix. When Father Gaufridi called on Jesus to help him, the demons answered through Madeleine:

> You are excellent at reciting the Litanies of the Sabbath. By God, you understand Lucifer; by Jesus Christ, Beelzebub; by the Holy Virgin, the apostate mother of Antichrist; by St. John the Baptist, the false prophet and precursor of Gog and Magog.
>
> —Eliphas Levi, *The History of Magic* (Boston: Weiser Books, 2001), p. 272

These blasphemous words terrified the exorcist. Father Gaufridi knew that this wild behavior couldn't be kept secret for long. Now he started to worry. How would the townspeople react when they realized that the devil was in their midst?

A Shocking Accusation

Father Gaufridi's exorcism failed, so he called in help. He turned to another priest who had experience imprisoning witches and other heretics during the Inquisition. His friend recommended that they bring in a new exorcist.

When the new priest failed, too, Father Gaufridi was ordered to try again. But this time, things were different. When Father Gaufridi entered the room with other priests, Sister Madeleine made a shocking accusation—Father Gaufridi himself was a follower of Satan. And other nuns were becoming possessed, too.

Faced with Sister Madeleine's claims and a convent full of possessed nuns, Father Gaufridi's friends turned against him. Now it was his turn to be questioned.

The Devil's Pact

Even though Sister Madeleine couldn't seem to stick to the same story for long, her case against the priest was detailed and convincing. She claimed that Father Gaufridi had fed her a charmed peach and seduced her when she was just a little girl. When Madeleine spoke in different voices, claiming she was the demon Beelzebub, people believed her. And when questioners touched her skin, they reported feeling the sensation of frogs writhing just beneath the surface.

МЫТАРСТВО

НА КОЕТО СЕ ИСТАЗВАТ КОНТ ЗАВИЖДА НА УЖДОТО ДОБРО, БРАТА СИ НЕНАВИДА Й ДРУГАГА СИ НЕ ЛЮБИ.

This fresco at a Bulgarian church, painted during the 1840s, shows Michael the Archangel defeating a group of demons in battle. Many Christians believe that angels and demons are able to interact with humans, though they are unseen, and that these supernatural creatures have an effect on everyday lives.

Father Gaufridi was thrown in a prison cell, tortured, and interrogated. Exhausted and deeply hurt, he was too weak to refuse to sign a confession in which he admitted to being a cannibal, a sorcerer, and friends with Satan himself. Even though he later tried to rescind the confession, his protests were futile. Sister Madeleine's behavior was proof that he had made a deal with the devil.

Madeleine's strange behavior continued throughout Father Gaufridi's trial. She told terrifying stories of her interactions with witches who fed the sacred Host to dogs and ate babies. Ashamed of

IS IT POSSESSION?

How can you tell if someone is possessed by a demon? For followers of the Roman Catholic faith, the answer has been clear since at least the 1500s, when *The Roman Ritual*, a book of official services for priests, was published. According to *The Roman Ritual*, there are four ways to determine if someone has been possessed by the devil:

1. They show superhuman strength, demonstrating physical power that does not match their physical size or capabilities. An exorcist must watch carefully for physical threats or face injury or death.

2. They speak in tongues, or languages they do not know or understand.

3. They know things they shouldn't know—information or knowledge that it would be impossible for them to know without being possessed by an outsider of some kind.

4. They experience "blasphemous rage," taking God's name in vain, falling down in violent fits, and avoiding or being repulsed by holy symbols, such as the cross, holy water, or the Bible.

But all devilish behavior isn't necessarily possession, and Catholics draw a line between people who have been possessed and people who have simply been affected by Satan. For example, someone who decides to give his life or his body over to the devil is not considered possessed, since possession happens against someone's will. And someone who is tempted by the devil or sees the devil at work through plagues or misfortunes is not possessed, either. And exorcists won't work with people who doctors determine are mentally ill.

her actions and worried about her own fate, she tried to commit suicide multiple times after people pointed to moles on her skin they claimed were the mark of the devil.

Persuaded by her detailed testimony, the jury decided that Gaufridi was indeed possessed and ordered his execution by burning. Now Madeleine became mute. She could not speak, hear, or see. Finally, she was thrown in prison herself.

THE AFTERMATH

The story of Sister Madeleine swept through Europe, setting people on edge. Could religious people be possessed by the devil? Were witchcraft and demon worship for real? Terrified, lawmakers decided to change their laws and accept the testimony of possessed people in court. Even today, the story of Sister Madeleine is seen as a sad example of what superstition, fear, and false accusations can do to a quiet community.

Most modern-day readers think that possessions and exorcisms are the stuff of horror movies, not real life. But that's only part of the truth. Humans have always believed in a world inhabited by good and evil spirits—and exorcisms are just one of a number of fascinating religious rituals that are still practiced today.

The religious rituals of yesterday and today may be eerie, complicated, and just plain strange, but they are all fascinating. They often reveal more than meets the eye. Religious rituals and beliefs shed light on how people see themselves and the world. And they might just change the way you think about everyday life.

ANGELS

Are angels really among us? Are these heavenly beings God's messengers or just a fantasy? Angels are the guardian spirits who some people think surround us at all times.

AN ANGELIC VICTORY

In 1914, eighty thousand British soldiers assembled on a French battlefield for one of the first battles of World War I. As they reached for their machine guns, confidence surged through the troops. The Germans didn't know who they were facing.

But over the course of the day, the battle began to go horribly wrong. Thousands of British forces were wounded or killed. The soldiers fell into formation again and again, but they couldn't seem to gain the upper hand against the relentless gunfire of the Germans.

Just as the British army started to retreat, something incredible happened. A strange cloud began to form. Silvery light poured over the battlefield.

Suddenly, arrows whizzed past the faces of the astonished soldiers.

The followers of many world religions, including Judaism, Christianity, and Islam, believe in supernatural beings called angels. They are considered to be good creatures who serve God and act as intermediaries between Heaven and Earth.

They realized that they were not alone: a group of medieval archers stood around them, protecting them with their bows and arrows. Who were these mysterious archers?

Terrified by the archers' assault, the German army began to draw back. The Battle of Mons was a huge comeback for the British. After the battle, soldiers began to tell the tale of the mysterious archers. It was even rumored that a German soldier had been found, pierced all over with arrow wounds. As news reached the home front, British people celebrated their victory and gave thanks to the angelic archers who helped protect their men.

Were the angels of Mons real? Some people think that the soldiers, hungry and exhausted from days of battle, must have hallucinated a force of friendly soldiers. Very few of the British soldiers who actually fought at Mons survived the war to re-tell the tale. In fact, the person who first wrote about the angels of Mons later said that he had made

Some of these British soldiers, who were wounded at the Battle of Mons in 1914, came to believe that a legion of angels had helped them to emerge victorious from the battle.

up the story. But many others remained convinced that the British victory at Mons was due to a group of angels sent from heaven.

MESSENGERS FROM HEAVEN

People of all religions and cultures believe in angels. Though the word angel means different things to different people, most people agree that it refers to a good-hearted or kind spirit that guards and guides humans.

Over thousands of years, angels have come to represent all that is good and holy. These divine creatures offer a glimpse of God on earth. And they can be found in religious traditions around the world.

From Christianity to Judaism, Islam to Sikhism, angels can be found in religious traditions and cultures the world over. In Kabbalah—Jewish mysticism—for example, it is believed that God sends angels to earth to perform specific tasks. Once the task is done, they vanish. Latter-Day Saints believe that all angels were people before they became spirits, or have yet to be born. And in Islam, angels have no free will; instead, they can only do what God commands.

A golden statue of the angel Moroni can be found on top of many temples of the Church of Jesus Christ of Latter-Day Saints (Mormons), including the Grand Temple in Salt Lake City. Moroni is one of the most recognizable symbols of the Mormon faith. According to legend, this angel gave the Book of Mormon to Joseph Smith.

ANCIENT ANGELS

The word *angel* comes from an ancient Hebrew term that means "messenger." In ancient times, people believed that angels were message bearers, spreading the word of the gods in the form of

In the Christian Bible, one of the most famous examples of an angel as God's messenger occurs in the Gospel of Luke, when the Angel Gabriel visits a young woman named Mary and tells her that she will conceive and bear a son. The event described in Luke 1: 26-39 has often been represented in Christian art throughout the ages.

prophecies and inspiring sacred texts. Over the years, messenger became messenger of God, as many religions focused on one deity. People started to name individual angels and associate them with different qualities and powers.

By the fifth century CE, angels were commonly associated with Christianity, even though nobody could seem to agree on just what an angel was. Was an angel a spiritual concept or a physical being? Who came first—angels or humans?

In 1215, a group of Catholic bishops weighed in on the debate. They decreed that God had created both angelic and earthly creatures before he created humanity. Angels did not have bodies or physical forms, the bishops said, but they were very real. The bishops also wrote for the first time about "fallen angels," spiritual beings who were created in innocence, but who turned their backs on the goodness with which they were born.

This proclamation helped bring angels into the mainstream. Angels began to appear in paintings, songs, and stories. People started to believe that all humans are surrounded by angels who care for them and ask God to protect and help them. As angels became more popular, more and more people reported real-life experiences with these heavenly messengers.

WINGS, HALOS, HARPS

Today, angels are as popular as ever. In fact, a 2014 survey conducted by the Gallup Organization found that 68 percent of all Americans believe in angels. People of different ages, genders, and religious con-

THE HIERARCHY OF ANGELS

Who's who in the world of angels? Over the years, Christians have developed a view of a carefully ordered hierarchy of angels, from God's right-hand men to angels assigned to lowly duties here on earth.

The traditional angel hierarchy has three spheres: heavenly counselors, heavenly governors, and heavenly soldiers. You'll find three different kinds of angels within each group.

First Sphere angels include seraphim (fiery caretakers of God's throne), cherubim (four-faced attendants of God), and thrones (carriers of God's will who appear in the form of wheels covered in eyes).

Second Sphere angels include dominions (angel lords with orbs of light), virtues (angels who supervise the sun, moon, and other heavenly bodies), and powers (warrior angels who make sure humans distribute power fairly).

Third Sphere angels include principalities (crown-wearing angels who look after groups of people, guard earth, and inspire humans), archangels (who guard nations and politics), and ordinary angels (who send messages to humans).

Each group of angels is also known as a "choir." Sometimes, they are even portrayed as an army ready to go to war for God—just like the angels of the Battle of Mons.

Depictions of angels decorate the ceiling of the Hagia Sophia, an ancient Muslim mosque in Turkey. In Islamic theology, two angels named Atid and Raqib are thought to write down every thought, feeling, and action of all humans throughout their lifetimes.

victions believe that angels exist. And pop culture has helped people imagine what angels might really look like.

Though pop culture portrayals of angels are growing more diverse every year, certain features have become shorthand for "angel." Most importantly, angels have wings. This wasn't always the case— Christian representations of angels didn't get wings until the fourth century CE. Some people see these wings as symbols of angels' nearness to heaven, while others believe that angels literally have wings and can fly.

The same holds true for the golden halo often pictured atop an angel's head. This custom seems to be a remnant of ancient portrayals of Biblical figures as having light surrounding their heads. Halos are depicted as auras, hovering rings, or even crowns.

And what about a golden harp? At some point, harps became associated with sacred music. No wonder many angels are never seen without a stringed instrument.

ANGELIC EXPERIENCES

Many people think of angels as the embodiment of a religious symbol or a myth. Others don't believe in them at all. But to some adherents of modern religions, angels are all too real. In fact, people have reported real-life angelic experiences for centuries.

In America, some studies suggest that up to 32 percent of people have seen or spoken to an angel. What's it like to see an angel? Reports vary.

It seems that not every angel appears with a halo and harp, clad in heavenly robes, and flapping impressive wings. Some people report seeing or talking to a being suffused with light or an invisible spirit. Others say that they have seen angels take the form of ordinary humans, like this woman, who felt angels in her midst when she was only five years old:

> My first experience happened when I was five years old and had a bad accident. I fell astride a manhole cover and had to be lifted off. When I got home from the hospital I slept with my parents for a while as I was really ill. In the middle of the night I awoke to find three "nuns" at the side of the bed. I woke my parents asking them why the nuns had come, but they could see nothing and told me to go back to sleep. The "nuns" remained with me until I fell asleep. I realized later that the "nuns" were angels protecting me and sending me healing. I am 59 now and have never forgotten my first angel experience.
>
> —Lesley Morgan, as quoted in Diana Cooper,
> *True Angel Stories: 777 Messages of Hope and Inspiration*

Zoroastrians believe that each person is assigned his or her own *fravashi*, or guardian angel. Four days after death, a person's spirit is believed to return to the angel who sent it to earth.

GUARDIANS AND GUIDES

Have you ever heard of a guardian angel? If so, you're not alone. One of the most common beliefs about angels is that they act as caretakers or guardians for particular individuals, protecting them from harm and accompanying them throughout their lifetimes. Guardian angels are said to guide their humans away from danger and help them make good decisions. Many people claim that they never would have survived an accident, made it through a tough time, or persevered through depression without their guardian angel by their side.

Some people associate angels with near-death experiences. A number of people who have experienced life-threatening accidents, surgeries, or other dangerous situations report that they have either seen or felt an angelic presence by their side. Others claim that their angel pushed them away from an oncoming car or caused their foot to stay

A statue of Michael the Archangel adorns a church in Kiev, Poland. The archangels are considered to be more powerful and important than ordinary angels, and are mentioned in the Bible and other scriptures. Christians believe that Michael will lead the forces of God in the final battle against evil, as described in the Book of Revelation. Other archangels include Gabriel and Raphael.

put when they were close to slipping off a cliff.

If you've ever felt torn between good and evil, you may be familiar with the idea of an angel on your shoulder. Popular culture often portrays people who are struggling to make a decision as consulting an angel on one shoulder and a devil on the other. The angel represents a person's ability to make wise decisions and act honestly. The devil represents temptation, impatience, and poor decision-making. Some people think that angels can help them make tough decisions and act as their best selves at all times.

Many people believe that guardian angels watch over them, keeping them from harm without being seen.

ARE ANGELS REAL?

So what about the victory in Mons? Were those angels real or imagined?

"The believability of the story was increased due to the semi-miraculous nature of the retreat against large odds of success," writes one historian in *The Encyclopedia of Religious Phenomena.* "The problem with the story . . . was its complete fiction. Published many months after the battle, [it was a] momentary distraction from a war that was not going well."

It turns out that not everyone believes in angels. Some doctors and psychologists claim that angelic experiences are nothing but hallucinations brought on by stress, fatigue, or mental disorders. Nonetheless, angels are more popular than ever. So hang up your halo and look over your shoulder—our culture's fascination with heavenly messengers isn't going anywhere anytime soon.

DEMONS

hat's the opposite of an angel? According to some religious beliefs, it's a demon—an evil, terrifying spirit that can control a person's body, mind, and life. Demons are fallen angels who threaten mayhem with their curses.

AN ANCIENT EXORCISM

Thousands of years ago, in a fishing village in ancient Israel, a stranger arrived in town. The man went to the local temple and started to preach, surprising the worshippers with his keen arguments and truthful manner. But suddenly, a man in the audience stood up and began shouting the preacher down. "Have you come to destroy us?" he yelled.

"Be quiet!" said the preacher. "Come out of him!" The man began to shake violently. In a few moments, a demon emerged from the body of the man in the audience, escaping with a horrific shriek. Amazed at the exorcism they had just witnessed, worshippers began to spread the word of Jesus of Nazareth, the man who had cast out a demon.

Modern images of demons as horned monsters are influenced by the deities worshiped by practitioners of ancient pagan religions. Some of the pagan fertility gods, such as the Canaanite god Baal, were depicted with horns or with the head of a goat or bull.

The Bible story of Jesus' exorcism at Capernaum is just one of hundreds of biblical tales relating to possession and evil spirits. Over two thousand years later, nearly every world religion and culture believes in the existence of some kind of demon.

EVIL AMONG US

The word *demon* is used to refer to any evil spirit. Manipulative, crafty, and just plain scary, demons are often blamed for bad behavior, violence, and the occult. Demons have come to symbolize the antisocial, scary forces at work in human nature, and are often used to explain bad luck and evil behavior.

But the word demon didn't always connote evil—in fact, the word used to refer to any kind of spirit, even a good one. Ancient people thought that the world was full of both kinds of spirits—forces responsible for earthly events and good and bad luck. Demons were known for their ability to inspire humans, animals, and even inanimate objects.

As time went on, the idea of demons evolved, right along with the idea of angels. People began to believe in specific demons that encouraged certain sins, like lust or murder. The notion of specific demons with evil powers came about just as the concept of the angel was becoming popular. If angels were designated to give God's messages and support humankind, people reasoned, there must also be spirits that worked against God. These rebel angels became known as "fallen angels," demons who had been kicked out of heaven for their evil deeds. Fallen angels weren't just evil—they were out for revenge.

THE PRINCE OF DARKNESS

The most famous fallen angel of all is Satan. Christians believe that Satan took the form of a serpent to tempt Eve in the Garden of Eden. God cast the serpent out of the garden and kicked Satan out of heaven, leading to an epic battle between good and evil that many Christians believe continues to this day.

Just as God rules heaven, Satan is believed to govern hell. Full of fire, pain, and tormenting demons, hell is the realm of evil, sin, and

There are several stories in the New Testament of the Christian Bible in which Jesus helps people who have been possessed by demons. The 18th century artwork here depicts the story in Matthew 8: 28-34, in which Jesus expels demons from a man and orders them to possess a nearby herd of pigs instead.

FAMOUS DEMONS

Books, movies and TV shows are full of famous demons. Do you recognize these evil figures?

Does the name Beelzebub ring a bell? He's one of the most famous fallen angels, and the word Beelzebub has become shorthand for Satan, the devil, or Lucifer. Beelzebub is known as the Lord of the Flies and is associated with the sin of pride. He is even thought to be responsible for jealousy, wars, and destruction.

But don't think that all demons are male. Lilith, a female demon from Jewish folklore and myth, was compared to a screech owl or a "night demon" in some texts. She is known for kidnapping and killing babies, seducing men and having demon babies with them, and even marrying Adam before he got together with Eve.

And don't mess around with an incubus. This male demon is thought to prey on women while they sleep so they will bear demonic children. The mythological wizard Merlin was supposedly the son of an incubus and a human woman. The female version of an incubus is a succubus—a demon who takes the form of a woman to destroy men in their dreams.

exclusion. This underworld is where sinners are tortured for their bad deeds—and Satan oversees all the evil action.

Satan is thought to rule over demons, witchcraft, black magic, and sin. Satan is often portrayed as reddish-colored, sporting hooves, horns, and a pitchfork. Satan is called the Prince of Lies and the ultimate enemy of good. He is known for his love of temptation and the hard bargains he makes for weak men's souls.

DEMON WORSHIP

According to a recent survey conducted by the Gallup Organization, 58 percent of Americans believe in the devil. And some people even worship Satan instead of God.

An organization called the Church of Satan was formed in the late 1960s and offers community, weddings, and even funerals to people who follow its tenets. Though it's not clear how many people actually belong to the Church of Satan, the group is known for satanic bap-

A man named Anton LaVey founded the Church of Satan in 1966. Its members claim that they are atheists who don't actually believe in demons, angels, or supernatural beings. According to the church website, adherents consider Satan a symbol of individualism, rather than a religious antagonist who requires sacrifice.

This pentagram includes a goat's head, a symbol of demonic activity. The names "Samael" and "Lilith" refer to demons from ancient mythology.

tisms, rituals, and masses. Veiled in secrecy, the Church of Satan even has its own Bible, which challenges the basic tenets of Christianity.

When news of the Church of Satan began to spread in the 1970s, people panicked. They accused Satanists of horrific ritual abuse, violence, and even murder. But even after over twelve thousand accusations and countless lawsuits and trials, nobody could prove that satanic ritual abuse was real. Yet openly practicing Satanists in the United States are few and far between.

POSSESSED BY THE DEVIL

One of the most frightening rumors about demons is that they can take over humans against their will. This phenomenon is called possession. Remember Sister Madeleine from chapter 1? She's just one example of a person whose behavior has led people to believe they have been taken over by the devil.

People who believe in possession tell tales of individuals who start to exhibit bizarre behavior and whose every action, word, and thought is dictated by evil spirits. And some of the symptoms of possession have to be seen to be believed: speaking in scary voices, having strange seizures, experiencing drastic changes in personality, revealing unusual wounds or injuries, or suddenly showing evidence of extraordinary or otherworldly knowledge.

Americans aren't the only people who believe in possession. Cultures on every continent have legends, traditions, and myths surrounding possession—and religious rituals to help rid a person of evil spirits. These practices are known as exorcism.

ALL ABOUT EXORCISM

Most of the world's major religions, including Islam, Christianity, Judaism, and Hinduism practice exorcism. In Islam, imams ask God for help and quote Qur'anic verses in a ritual thought to be medicinal in nature. In Judaism, a rabbi and a group of ten men form a circle

The exorcism of demons is described in the Dead Sea Scrolls, some of the oldest manuscripts on earth.

Gargoyles are demonic-appearing creatures that were used to decorate the outside of many Christian churches in Europe during the Middle Ages. It was believed that the grotesque figures would protect the church from evil spirits. Gargoyles like these examples from the famous Notre Dame Cathedral in Paris had a functional purpose as well: they are waterspouts connected to a system of gutters and they protect the cathedral by keeping rainwater away so it can't damage the structure.

around the person thought to be possessed. After reciting Psalm 91 three times in a row, the rabbi blows a ram's horn to shake the devil loose. In Hinduism, people recite mantras over the person suspected of being possessed and make offerings with incense to drive devils away.

If you associate exorcism with a priest holding up a cross and commanding demons to leave someone's body, you're probably thinking of the Roman Catholic rite of exorcism. The practice of exorcism in Christian faiths is as old as Christianity itself—Jesus reportedly performed exorcisms and cast out demons during his lifetime. Nowadays, exorcisms are actually quite rare, and can only be performed by an experienced priest in the presence of family members or other witnesses.

"A demon can't control a person's soul; it can only control a person's body," said Father Gary Thomas, a priest who performs exorcisms in San Jose, California. When possession is suspected, a priest first works with doctors and mental health professionals to determine if a person is really possessed. Then, he gets permission from his bishop to conduct the exorcism. Finally, the priest confronts the demon, using ritual prayers and continuing to pray and perform the ritual over and over again until the exorcism succeeds.

"You know the exorcism is over when the manifestations stop," says Father Thomas. "But you don't stop the prayers immediately, because the demons will try to trick you into thinking they've left when they haven't. So when the manifestations end, you continue for a serious period of time praying the rite, and when there's no more, then you have to make a judgment as to whether they've left. And you also ask the person, 'Do you sense anything within you?' So you rely on them to some degree, and you rely on what you're observing"

People have reported strange occurrences during exorcisms, from levitating objects to terrifying attacks to a chill that fills the room. The exorcist doesn't just pray: he commands demons to leave their victim. When the rite is over, the victim is often drained, but relieved.

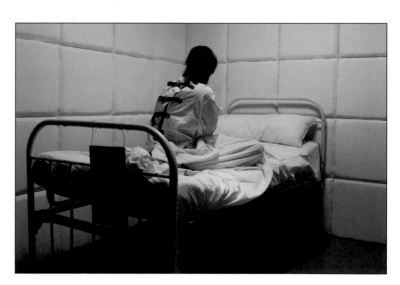

Though some people with mental illness think or act like they are possessed by demons, possession is not a diagnosis used by doctors or psychiatrists.

Ogoh-ogoh are large statues built each year for observation of the Hindu festival of Nyepi in Bali, Indonesia. Statues are paraded through each local town, then burned to symbolize purification of the community and drive away evil spirits.

GOOD VERSUS EVIL

Those who believe in exorcisms claim that an exorcism is the ultimate battle of good versus evil. But others don't buy that. Psychologists have raised concerns that people thought to be possessed may be mentally or physically ill and that exorcism and accusations of possession can be used as a weapon against people who act strangely or look different than other people in their communities. Others claim that people who show signs of possession are not sick at all, but are susceptible to superstition or suggestion or are seeking attention and care from others.

Regardless of what you believe about exorcism, you might encounter the subject when you pick up a thriller or horror story or watch a scary movie. Movies like *The Exorcist* and *The Rite* have been causing people to fall out of their seats in fear for decades. These pop culture exorcisms sometimes create the misconception that possession and exorcism are everywhere. Hardly. Most religious communities take possession and exorcism extremely seriously and do everything in their power to avoid accusing people of possession.

There's a name for the practice of using magical ceremonies to summon demons: goetia, *from the ancient Greek word for "charm" or "spell." Some modern occult practitioners claim that they have invoked demons through their spells and rituals.*

ANCIENT RELIGIOUS RITUALS

From mummies to ritual killings, curses to strange ceremonies, ancient religious rituals can be both scary and fascinating. And the ancient world offered plenty of ways to celebrate and worship the gods and goddesses.

HUMAN SACRIFICE AMONG THE ANCIENT MAYANS

Murder is a sin in most cultures, and for good reason. If we didn't have bans on killing other people, it would be hard for any culture or religion to survive! But in the Mayan civilization in Mesoamerica, religion and murder went hand in hand, due to a strong tradition of ritual human sacrifice.

Ancient Mayans thought that the gods needed blood for nourishment, and human blood was the best blood of all. Ancient Mayan texts, artworks, and legends tell the tale of thousands of murders on behalf of the hungry gods—and huge burial grounds and archaeological digs prove that human sacrifice was an important part of Mayan culture.

Sound grisly? It gets worse. Not only did Mayans sacrifice humans,

This temple at the ancient Mayan city of Tikal was one of many sites throughout Central America and Mexico where the Mayans made regular sacrifices to their gods. Often, enemies captured in warfare were the victims of these grisly rituals.

Like the Maya, the Aztecs of Mesoamerica believed in human sacrifice as a key element of their religion. In this drawing from an ancient Aztec codex, a priest holds the bleeding heart of a sacrifice victim aloft to the god Huitzilopochtli. Another victim lies at the foot of the altar. The Aztecs believed Huitzilopochtli, the sun god, needed sacrifices of human blood in order to climb into the sky to start each new day. Without regular sacrifice, the sun would not rise and the world would end.

but they did so in extremely brutal ways. From decapitation to death by bow and arrow to being thrown into a hole or buried alive, there were plenty of ways to sacrifice a Mayan to the gods.

But perhaps the creepiest aspect of Mayan human sacrifice will hit you right in the heart. That's right. Some human sacrifices in Mayan culture involved a priest reaching into the victim's chest cavity to offer a still-beating heart to the gods.

"The Maya had a complex relationship with the underworld, and their conception of it was quite different from the Christian concept of hell," explains author Stanislav Chladek in his book *Exploring Maya Ritual Caves: Dark Secrets from the Maya Underworld.* "Maya religious beliefs were permeated with belief in an afterlife, which could take place only after the dead passed through the trials of Xibalba, ruled by the Lords of the Underworld, Xibalbans. Ever-present death led the Maya to dedicate much of their ritual to this final confrontation with the underworld's lords and their own eventual rebirth."

READY FOR SACRIFICE

Human sacrifice may sound unthinkable today, but it was a key element in Mayan culture. However, only the elite were sacrificed. People from lower classes who were captured during battles were denied the honor of human sacrifice and turned into slaves instead.

An ancient Mayan would be shocked to hear that some people would never commit murder for the sake of religion. Records show that Mayans were happy to be selected for sacrifice. People who were sacrificed for the gods were thought to go straight to heaven.

But Mayan sacrifice was child's play compared to the Aztecs in Mexico, who are thought to have sacrificed as many as fourteen people per minute during some bloody festivals.

CURSES IN ANCIENT GREECE AND ROME

Have you ever wished bad luck would befall someone you didn't like? If you lived in ancient Greek and Roman times, you wouldn't have been satisfied with mere resentment. You would have taken action by calling on the gods to curse your enemy.

When archaeologists began to excavate Greek and Roman ruins, they often discovered something unusual: hundreds of small sheets of lead that had been written on, then buried, hidden, or thrown away. These artifacts became known as "curse tablets." Anthropologists now believe they served an important purpose in ancient culture.

Curse tablets were used to record grievances, prayers, or just names in the hopes that the gods would listen and punish the author's enemies. Some curse tablets don't contain curses at all—rather, they contain information about court cases or even spells intended to make another person fall in love.

The jury is still out on exactly why people used curse tablets. Were

The ancient Roman baths in the United Kingdom were built more than 2,000 years ago, but were covered over and unknown until they were accidentally discovered in the late 1800s. Today, they are a major tourist attraction and historic site.

they just a way to vent without confronting another person? Were they the ancient equivalent of uttering some swear words? Either way, they were definitely popular—thousands of curse tablets have been found around the world, showing centuries of ill will toward others.

THE CURSES OF BATH

For hundreds of years, people have visited the springs of Bath, England, to bathe in the city's hot springs and spas. But archaeologists found over one hundred artifacts that could ruin anyone's spa day: Roman curse tablets carved with messages of revenge and hatred. The tablets were carved over the course of two centuries (between 200 and 400 CE) and tell an incredible story of thievery.

When people visited the baths, their clothing, jewelry, or other personal possessions were often stolen. Angry and anxious for revenge, people would carve their complaints on curse tablets and dedicate them to the goddess Minerva. Then they would throw them into the hot springs or nail them on the wall of the bathhouses.

But even though bathhouse theft seems to have been commonplace, that didn't stop people from seething with revenge when their stuff got snatched. One curse tablet reads, "Docimedis has lost two gloves and asks that the thief responsible should lose their minds [sic] and eyes in the goddess' temple." That's a pretty serious punishment for stealing a pair of gloves!

Curse tablets were thin pieces of lead that was inscribed with a message, then folded over several times. The message often asked the gods to do bad things to people who harmed or stole from the writer.

The curse tablets aren't just an amazing record of an ancient religious ritual—they're important historical documents, too. Archaeologists prize them as one-of-a-kind documents that show the use of the British Celtic language and even the earliest use of the word Christian in England.

MUMMIES IN ANCIENT EGYPT

If you're looking for complicated or creepy rituals, you need look no further than how a culture deals with their dead. That's the case for ancient Egyptians, who will forever be associated with their desire to preserve their dead for all eternity. Egyptian mummies might seem a bit gross, but they're also a fascinating tool for understanding how ancient people saw the world.

What's a mummy? The word is used to refer to any corpse that has been preserved. In Egypt, hot and dry conditions in shallow mass graves led to the accidental mummification of buried bodies. Once Egyptians realized that their dead were being preserved, they began to mummify people on purpose.

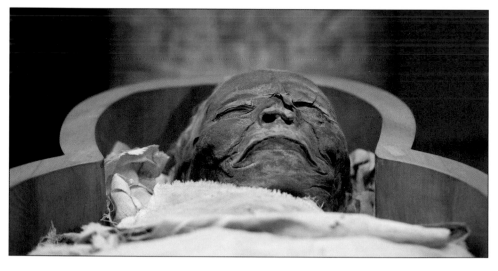

The ritual for preparing a mummy in ancient Egypt took about 70 days from start to finish. The process was often changed and refined over the 3,000 years that Egyptians mummified their dead, but the basic elements remained the same: removing the internal organs, removing moisture from the corpse, and applying a protective covering of resin and bandages.

Egyptians believed that the afterlife was of supreme importance. Being turned into a mummy became a way to ensure that you'd live well in the next world. And the Egyptians developed an amazingly complex set of tools and rituals as they buried their dead.

First, a corpse was prepared for mummification. All organs except for the heart were removed and the body was washed down with a potent mix of wine and ritual spices. Over the next forty days, the mummy would be dehydrated and wrapped in cloth. The mummy would be coated in resin, sealed inside a coffin, and laid in a sealed tomb, along with amulets, food, and possessions for the afterlife.

DEATH AS LIFE

As ancient Egyptians got better at making mummies, they became more and more obsessed with death. Simple funerals became elaborate parties that involved dancing, dining, and creating incredible works of art to honor the dead. The richer you were in life, the more elaborate your funeral, mummification, and burial were once you were dead.

Egyptians believed that the dead still participated in the lives of the living and that the spirits of the dead could help people through life. It's no wonder, then, that they found death and funeral customs to be so important. Egyptian burial artifacts are among the world's most prized pieces of art.

When European explorers began to spend more time in Egypt, they were astonished to find temples, pyramids, and burial sites packed with priceless artifacts and plenty of mummies. Unfortunately, the obsession with Egyptian culture that followed led to some terrible consequences for Egypt's precious culture and arti-

Even though human sacrifice is now against the law around the world, during the last decade human sacrifices have been illegally performed in Liberia, India, Bangladesh, and even the United Kingdom. In 2001 police in London found the torso of a West African boy floating in the Thames River. He had been ritually murdered as a sacrifice to some unknown deity.

facts. People raided tombs, stole art and mummies, and ransacked burial sites without regard to their cultural significance. Egyptians are still recovering stolen funeral artifacts to this day.

Today, Egyptologists use the work of ancient writers, as well as modern technology, to learn more about the Egyptian mummification process and the culture in which it existed. Historians of the ancient world, such as the Roman writer Herodotus who visited Egypt around 450 BCE, have told modern scientists most of what is known about the actual process of mummification. The development of computerized scanning equipment and x-rays now makes it possible to examine mummies without destroying the elaborate outer wrappings. By autopsies on mummified bodies, experts learn more about diseases suffered by the ancient Egyptians, as well as the treatment for those illnesses. Bones can provide clues about everyday life in ancient Egypt, including diet and lifespan.

THE BULL FEAST AMONG ANCIENT CELTIC TRIBES

Religion and rulers don't always mix, but in ancient Celtic society, a religious ceremony helped people figure out who should lead them. The Tarbhfhess ceremony, or Bull Feast, used a sacred animal to help people identify their next leader.

In some ancient civilizations, the bull was a strong animal only owned by wealthy and powerful people. Celts used it to select the most powerful man in their culture: the king. The festival that developed became known as the Bull Feast or Bull Sleep.

When a man was chosen to be king, he had to prove his worthiness through a number of tests and religious rituals. During the feast, tribesmen would figure out if their chosen king was really the chosen one. They would choose a person to participate in the ritual and help

The Celts aren't the only culture to celebrate the bull: the Running of the Bulls in Pamplona, Spain, is an annual festival that attracts over one million spectators each year.

him slaughter a bull. After killing the bull, the participant drank its blood and ate its meat until he was full. Then he would lie down and go to sleep, lulled into dreams by the chants of four Druid priests who accompanied him. If the man saw the proposed king in his dream, the tribesmen knew that the gods approved of their selection.

Examining your dreams after feasting on a bull may not be the most efficient way to choose a political leader, but for ancient Celts it served an important purpose. Not only did the ritual allow people to think over the appropriateness of their proposed leader for the position of king, but the ceremony made use of a precious bull, an animal that signified prosperity, wealth, and power. Those are all attributes you want in a ruler.

Animal Worship

The Celts weren't the only ancient people who worshiped animals. In fact, almost every nation and culture has animals they consider to be sacred.

Hindus in Nepal and some areas of India consider dogs to be religious figures. The festival of Tihar is a five-day celebration of animals, including dogs. During Tihar, dogs are dressed up with a red forehead dot and a garland of bright yellow marigolds, and are covered in incense. Why the special treatment? Dogs are thought to serve as divine messengers and even guard the gates of heaven.

For the indigenous Tlingit people of Alaska, the raven has special religious significance. Ravens are rumored to have created the earth after dropping a stone into the ocean. You can find images of ravens on canoes, on totem poles, and in Tlingit homes.

Elephants are worshiped in Thailand, where believers suspect that white elephants carry the spirit of the Buddha. People consider elephants to bring good luck and build shrines to the god Ganesh, a half-man, half-elephant god.

Do you like cats? So did the ancient Egyptians. Not only did they worship a cat god, but they mummified cats and buried them in elaborate tombs. Ancient historians have written that people in Egypt mourned cats as loudly as if they were human.

MODERN RELIGIOUS RITUALS

Think religious rituals ended with ancient culture? Think again. Strange and intriguing rituals are alive and well in modern times. Rituals like firewalking, worshipping saints, avoiding pork, and celebrating with the dead put a modern twist on ancient beliefs.

FIREWALKING IN HINDUISM

Would you walk across a bed of burning-hot coals with your bare feet? If you're brave enough to answer yes, you're not alone. Firewalking, a religious ritual in which people walk barefoot over burning coals, embers, or hot stones to prove their faith, has been practiced since at least 1200 BCE.

Why on earth would people subject themselves to this dangerous feat? During the Hindu festival of Thimithi, believers go through a fiery religious ritual that's all about bravery, truthfulness, and faith. And the peak of the festival takes a real leap of faith as the devoted walk slowly across red-hot coals.

The festival is based on a Hindu tale of the goddess Draupadi, a

A priest walks on hot coals during a celebration of the Hindu festival of Thimithi in Thailand. This unusual practice originated as a religious ritual in the Indus Valley more than 3,000 years ago.

Hindus in India are not the only people who practice firewalking as part of their religious beliefs. People in Indonesia, Japan, Fiji, and throughout southeastern Asia have incorporated this ritual into their own religious festivals.

mythical queen who walked across hot coals to prove her faith and purity. Legend has it that anyone who is as pure as Draupadi can walk across the hot coals at the Thimithi festival without being burned. During the festival, believers reenact Draupadi's trial by fire with a series of elaborate rituals and rites.

The Thimithi festival lasts for a week. After a period of prayer, participants reenact Draupadi's marriage to Arjuna and simulate a human sacrifice. Then, people carrying pots of milk perform a special walk, pausing to pray and bow after every single step. Some people roll around the grounds of the temple to prove their faithfulness. A statue of Mariamman, the Hindu mother goddess, is bathed in the milk to help wash human sins away and participants hold a parade that reenacts a historic battle.

WALKING THROUGH FIRE

Finally, a fire pit is prepared. A priest kicks off the firewalking by moving slowly through the fire pit while balancing a pot of water on his head. From dawn until nearly midnight on the last day of the festival, believers walk through the fire pit to prove their faith and devotion.

One trick to firewalking is to allow the fire to burn until a layer of gray ash coats the coals. The ash helps insulate the walker's feet from the blazing temperatures. Still, you have to walk quickly to keep from being burned. No running, though, because that drives the feet through the ash into the hottest part of the fire!

Is it possible to walk across hot coals without hurting yourself? Yes. Many people who walk through fire do not burn their feet at all. The physics of temperature and heat conductivity help protect feet from hot coals in certain circumstances.

But don't grab your matches just yet. In order to get through a firewalking ceremony without getting burned, you must walk through the fire at just the right pace. Running makes it more likely that you will get burned. No wonder this ceremony is among the scariest in the world.

SAINTS IN MODERN CATHOLICISM

Have you ever heard someone refer to another person as a "saint"? The term doesn't just refer to people who are extremely good, patient, or kind—the word *saint* refers to someone who has been dubbed espe-

Did you lose something? You might want to pray to St. Anthony, the patron saint of lost things. Saint Anthony of Padua was a Portuguese priest and member of the Franciscan order who lived in the thirteenth century.

cially holy within their religion. And though many religions have recognized holy figures, the Catholic system of saints is uniquely complicated and fascinating.

The idea of saints has been around since people began to interact with one another in ancient times. Just as in modern times, the good deeds or kind acts of some individuals stood out from the pack. People told and retold tales of these people's virtuous acts.

Over time, people began to think that these extraordinary people were special indeed. Not only did their lives exemplify good ideals and religious virtues, according to this view, but they must be smiled on by God. People started to worship their deeds and ask the saints for special attention and favors.

In the tenth century CE, Catholic popes began to recognize extraordinary individuals and proclaim them to be saints. The first saint, Bishop Ulrich of Augsburg, was canonized by Pope John XV in the

Pope John Paul II, leader of the Roman Catholic Church from 1978 until his death in 2005, played an important role in world affairs. He was beatified in 2009, and canonized, or declared a saint, in 2014.

The Archangel Gabriel appears to the prophet Daniel in this stained-glass window artwork from the cathedral in Brussels, Belgium. The name Gabriel means "God has shown Himself mighty." Gabriel appears many times in the Bible, generally bringing messages from God.

year 993. Over time, the church implemented a system called "beatifi-cation." This process finds potential saints and puts them through a series of steps to verify that they are worthy of being called a saint, or "canonized."

BECOMING A SAINT

The process of canonizing a saint has changed over the years, becom-ing more formal and taking potential saints from normal person to saint with heavenly privileges. Once potential saints are nominated, bishops investigate their life and works to see if they are worthy of moving forward in the process. First, they are called "servants of God." Then, the pope declares them to be "venerable" or "heroic in virtue." Then, if the pope and the investigative team find that a miracle was performed by the saint or they were killed for their faith, they are beatified and given the name "blessed." If two miracles are associated with each of the beatified people, they are named a saint and given a feast day. People often worship saint nominees, but churches cannot be built in their honor until they have been canonized.

Once a saint is canonized, he or she joins a long list of religious figures who are given special devotion by some Catholics. People can ask a saint to put in a good word for them with God, help them heal or accomplish a particular task, protect them throughout their lifetimes, or bless a particular group or profession.

KNOW YOUR SAINTS

Catholics aren't the only people who worship saints. Many modern holidays center around the feast days of popular saints.

St. Valentine's Day (February 14) has come a long way from its religious roots. The festival honors St. Valentine, who is thought to have performed forbidden weddings for Christian believers who were jailed by the Romans. Nowadays, Valentine's Day is a love feast featuring romantic notes and cards, candy, roses, and plenty of hearts.

St. Patrick's Day (March 17) celebrates the life of Ireland's patron saint. Over the years, the day has become a party in honor of Irish heritage. Plenty of non-Irish people dress up in green, eat Irish soda bread and corned beef, and cry "Erin go bragh" ("Ireland forever") at parades and parties.

All Hallows' Eve (October 31) is known as Halloween in the United States. This popular holiday is a time for tricks and treats, candy and costumes, and plenty of spooky surprises. It's also the lead-up to All Saint's Day on November 1, a day to honor saints and the dead.

St. Nicholas Day (December 6) is a big festival in many European countries that use the day to celebrate the man who inspired Santa Claus. Children set out shoes overnight and awaken to find them filled with gifts, trinkets, and funny poems.

PORK TABOO IN JUDAISM AND ISLAM

Food is ripe with ritual—there are traditions baked into every meal you eat. And one of the most widely practiced religious rituals of all is the avoidance of pork or pork products. What's wrong with pork? It depends on who you ask.

For example, Jews believe that God forbade them to eat animals with cloven or split hooves, which includes pigs. Jews who follow traditional dietary laws and keep kosher believe that pork is unclean and unholy. To connect their daily lives more closely to their religious faith, they avoid consuming any pork or pork products.

The laws of *kashrut* (that is, keeping kosher) also regulate the preparation and serving of food and require that meat and dairy products cannot be prepared or consumed at the same time. Similarly, Islamic laws designate certain foods as *halal* (lawful) and others as *haram* (against the law). The Qur'an states that Allah forbids people from eating pork, but will forgive those who must eat it. *Halal* prac-

Observant Jews are careful to follow kosher laws related to food preparation, even when it comes to purchasing fast food. This restaurant is located in Tel Aviv, Israel.

tices regulate the slaughter, preparation, and consumption of all foods eaten by Muslims, just as kosher laws do for Jews.

Though pork avoidance is religious in nature, historians think that it may have served an important purpose for ancient people: protecting people's health and wealth. Some historians speculate that people started avoiding pork to reduce diseases contracted by pigs' scavenging ways. Others theorize that ancient cultures that forbid the consumption of pork did so because keeping pigs cost too much money and was ecologically unsustainable. Still others think that the reasoning behind avoiding pork has nothing to do with health, but rather that pork meat is just a bit too close to the texture, color, and flavor of human flesh.

DÍA DE LOS MUERTOS IN MEXICO

If you're anything like many Americans, you may hold your breath or walk more quickly when you pass a cemetery. Our culture sees death as creepy, terrifying, and morbid. But in Mexico, an important fall festival celebrates death—and takes place inside graveyards themselves. Día de los Muertos, or Day of the Dead, is the name of a three-day Mexican celebration that occurs from October 31 to November 2 each year. The celebration is known for its elaborate artwork and rituals that honor the dead and keep their memory alive all year long.

The Day of the Dead tradition has been around for nearly three thousand years. It originated in Aztec culture, where people remembered and celebrated the deaths of their ancestors. Now, people who celebrate the Day of the Dead get together in cemeteries on Halloween and the days that follow to offer food and decorations to the dead, visit their ancestors' graves, and celebrate the lives of their loved ones.

Though every individual celebrates the Day of the Dead differently, the holiday is associated with several colorful traditions. The most

Mexicans use bright golden-colored marigolds to honor the dead at Día de Muertos (Day of the Dead) gatherings.

Members of a mariachi band perform during a Day of the Dead service in a cemetery in Aguascalientes, Mexico.

common is the decoration of cemeteries. Families gather at graveyards to maintain, spruce up, and decorate their loved ones' graves with flowers, altars and shrines, and gifts of toys and food.

During the three-day celebration, people visit with relatives, neighbors, and friends; tell stories; and have picnics at their loved ones' graves, leaving offerings of food and flowers to tempt departed souls to celebrate along with them. People dress up in skull masks and make and eat elaborately decorated sugar skulls.

It might seem strange to celebrate death instead of mourning it, but Día de los Muertos is a chance for people to catch up with their friends and neighbors, remember their loved ones, and help ensure

For the Day of the Dead, Mexicans decorate altars with sugar skulls, foods that deceased relatives liked, specially baked bread, alcoholic drinks, marigolds, photographs, and candles.

that the dead are part of the community long after they have finished walking the earth. Far from being a scary or morbid holiday, Día de los Muertos characterizes death as a crucial part of a person's life cycle—and it does so with colorful costumes, decorations, dance, food, and song.

WHY WE NEED RITUALS

From ancient rites to modern religious practices, it's clear that humans love to participate in rituals. But why? Can rituals change the way we feel, think, or act?

Some scientists think so. In an article in the *Journal of Experimental Psychology*, scientists Francesca Gino and Michael I. Norton write that rituals can have positive impacts, regardless of how they're performed. They proved this in experiments done with people who had lost a loved one, broken up with a partner, or lost the lottery.

In their experiment, Gino and Norton found that rituals increased feelings of control and reduced feelings of grief—even for people who did not believe the rituals would work. The ritual itself didn't matter much (the study included practices from religion, everyday rituals, and ones made up on the spot). Instead, the fact that people performed any kind of ritual at all is what seemed to count. The scientists concluded that no matter what the ritual, ritual behaviors serve a common purpose: they help us regain a sense of control over our lives.

FINDING COMMON GROUND

Think you don't need rituals? You're probably wrong. Every time you say a prayer, shake someone's hand, or cross your fingers, you're performing a ritual.

Rituals are all around us, from the food we eat to the way we see good and evil. And the more you look at religious rituals, the more similarities you see across cultures. From angels to demons, special meals to elaborate feasts, we can all find common ground in our need to celebrate, question, and explore together.

CHRONOLOGY

3400 BCE   Egyptians begin to mummify their dead.

1200 BCE   The practice of firewalking becomes popular among cultures in the the Indus Valley, and soon spreads to other parts of Asia.

ca. 30 CE   During his public ministry, which lasts for about three years, Jesus of Nazareth drives demons out of several afflicted people.

ca. 200   Romans use curse tablets in hopes of gaining revenge on their enemies. The tablets are often left in shrines to various deities in places like Bath, England.

ca. 250   Mayans begin to sacrifice humans.

ca. 300   Christian artists begin to depict angels with wings.

1215   At a synod, or meeting of the entire Roman Catholic church hierarchy, bishops officially define the nature of angels.

1521   After conquering the Aztec empire of Mexico, Spanish rulers outlaw the Aztec religion, including human sacrifices, and force natives to convert to Christianity.

1610   The episode known as the Aix-en-Provence Possession occurs, in which a nun named Sister Madeleine is believed to be possessed by a demon. Eventually, Father Louis Gaufridi was convicted of devil worship by the inquisition, and burned at the stake.

1614	The Roman Catholic Church publishes *Rituale Romanum* ("The Roman Ritual"), a book that includes the ritual for exorcising demons.
1914	According to a published story, some British soldiers report seeing angelic archers at the Battle of Mons. Although the story's author later says he made it up, some veterans do come forth to say the appearance actually happened, and it passes into British military lore.
1949	Priests perform an exorcism on a Maryland boy known as "Roland Doe." The case would inspire the 1973 film *The Exorcist,* which is still considered one of the scariest movies of all time
1966	The Church of Satan is founded by Anton LaVey, who goes on to write many books about Satanism, including *The Satanic Bible.*
1999	The Roman Catholic Church publishes an updated version of the exorcism ritual.
2001	A child's torso, with the head, arms, and legs cut off in a ritual fashion, is discovered in the Thames River in London. Investigators eventually determine that the child, a five-year-old West African boy, was killed as part of a human sacrifice ritual.
2008	Mexico's Day of the Dead celebrations are included in UNESCO's Representative List of the Intangible Cultural Heritage of Humanity.
2014	A study by the Gallup Organization finds that 68 percent of Americans believe in angels, while 58 percent believe in the devil.

GLOSSARY

amulet—an object used for protection against evil spirits or demons.

angel—a spiritual being believed to act as God's messenger on earth.

archangel—according to Judaism, Christianity, and Islam, this is a high-ranking or particularly important angel. Three notable examples are Michael, Gabriel, and Raphael.

choir—a group of angels.

curse—a phrase that calls on gods or spirits to punish or cause harm to another person.

demon—an evil spirit or devil.

demonology—the study of demons.

exorcism—a ritual in which demons are cast out of a possessed person.

goetia—a magical practice in which a person attempts to invoke, or summon, a demon.

human sacrifice—the practice of killing people as offerings to the gods.

incantation—a chant or spell that uses words.

invoke—an appeal to someone or something, such as an angel or demon, for help, protection, or power.

Kabbalah—an ancient Jewish tradition of interpreting and understanding the scriptures through mystical rituals.

mummy—a preserved human corpse wrapped in bandages.

near-death experience—an unusual experience that occurs when a person is on the brink of death, but recovers. Often, people describe the feeling of leaving their body, seeing angels, or moving toward a tunnel of light.

possession—the takeover of a person's mind and body by an evil spirit.

priest—a religious leader.

ritual—a ceremony or rite.

saint—a holy person thought to reside in heaven.

Sikhism—a monotheistic religion founded in northern India during the 15th century. Today it is considered the fifth-largest organized religion in the world, with about 30 million followers.

taboo—something forbidden or looked down on.

Zoroastrianism—a monotheistic religion founded in Persia more than 2,600 years ago. Although it was nearly wiped out by the rise of Islam in the Middle East during the seventh and eighth centuries ce, about 2 million people worldwide still follow Zoroastrian precepts today.

FURTHER READING

The Encyclopedia of Religious Phenomena. Canton, Mich.: Visible Ink Press, 2008.

Guiley, Rosemary Ellen. *The Encyclopedia of Angels*. New York: Checkmark Books, 2004.

Lasky, Kathy. *Days of the Dead*. Great Neck, N.Y.: StarWalk Kids Media, 2014.

Mack, Carol K. and Dinah. *A Field Guide to Demons, Fairies, Fallen Angels, and Other Subversive Spirits*. New York: Little, Brown & Co., 1998.

Putnam, James. *Mummy*. New York: DK Eyewitness Books, 2009.

INTERNET RESOURCES

www.angelmuseum.org

Visit the site of the Angel Museum, a museum boasting the world's largest collection of angelic art.

www.penn.museum/long-term-exhibits/the-egyptian-mummy.html

Find out about mummies and even see how mummies get CAT-scanned at the Penn Museum's Egyptian Mummy display on the museum site.

www.smithsonianmag.com/videos/category/smithsonian-channel/the-devil-on-the-inside/?no-ist

Watch a video from the Smithsonian, called "The Devil on the Inside," about the possession that inspired *The Exorcist*.

www.worldmuseumofman.org/mayan2.php?collection = TRUE

View tools used for human sacrifice in ancient Mayan culture at the World Museum of Man's Pre-Columbian Collection.

www.metmuseum.org/collection/the-collection-online/search/435725

Learn about a famous painting, "Christ's Descent into Hell," which depicts Satan and the horrors of hell.

INDEX

Numbers in **bold italic** refer to captions.

ABOUT THE AUTHOR

Audrey Alexander's award-winning nonfiction has taken her to 1840s England, 1940s Amsterdam, and ancient Greece. She has lived in Massachusetts, California, Colorado, and Germany. When she's not curled up with a book, you'll find her roller-skating, singing, or working on the perfect green chile stew.